ANTHONY HOROWITZ

CREATOR OF ALEX RIDER

Cath Senker

Published in 2013 by Wayland
Copyright © Wayland 2013

Wayland
338 Euston Road
London NW1 3BH

Wayland Australia
Level 17/207 Kent Street
Sydney, NSW 2000

Editor: Debbie Foy
Designer: Paul Cherrill for Basement68

British Library Cataloguing in
Publication Data
 Senker, Cath.
Anthony Horowitz. -- (Inspirational lives)
  1. Horowitz, Anthony,
  1955- --Juvenile literature.
  2. Authors, English--20th century
  --Biography--Juvenile literature.
I. Title II. Series
823.9'2-dc23

ISBN: 978 0 7502 7873 7

Printed in China

10 9 8 7 6 5 4 3 2 1

Wayland is a division of Hachette
Children's Books, an Hachette UK
company.
www.hachette.co.uk

Picture acknowledgments: The author
and publisher would like to thank the
following for allowing their pictures to be
reproduced in this publication: Cover:
© Chris Jackson/Getty Images; 4: Oxford
© David Levenson/Getty Images; 5: MGM
/Everett/ Rex Features; 6: © Anthony
Horowitz; 7: © Maurice Savage/Alamy; 8:
Bonnie Jacobs/iStock; 9: SuperStock
/Getty Images; 10: image provided by
Rugby School, founded in 1567; 11: ©
Peter Walton Photography/Getty Images;
12: PA/PA Archive/Press Association
Images; 13: © David Farrell/Getty Images;
14: Groosham Grange, cover designs ©
Walker Books Ltd; 15 © ITV/Rex Features;
16: © Mark Anstead/Rex Features; 17:
© Dave Hogan/Getty Images; 18: ©
Ian West/PA Archive/Press Association
Images; 19: © Grant Archive/TopFoto; 20:
Point Blanc cover designs © Walker Books
Ltd; 21: © The Washington Post/Getty
images; 22: Raven's Gate cover designs ©
Walker Books Ltd; 23: © ITV/Rex Features;
24: © Gary Lee/UPPA/Photoshot; 25: ©
Gamma-Rapho via Getty Images; 26: ©
Steve Parsons/PA Wire/Press Association
Images; 27: © RNIB world reading day –
with kind permission from RNIB; 28: ©
Ray Tang/Rex Features; 29: © Starstock/
Photoshot.

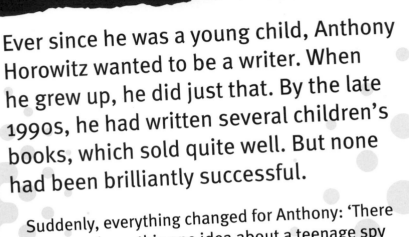

Ever since he was a young child, Anthony Horowitz wanted to be a writer. When he grew up, he did just that. By the late 1990s, he had written several children's books, which sold quite well. But none had been brilliantly successful.

Suddenly, everything changed for Anthony: 'There had always been this one idea about a teenage spy that had been nudging at my consciousness, and one afternoon I sat down and wrote the first sentence of what was to be *Stormbreaker*, the opening novel in the Alex Rider series.' He just knew this book would be special.

TOP TIP

Ideas for stories can come from all kinds of places. You might hear fascinating snippets of conversations on the bus or train, so always keep your ears open and a notebook handy.

Anthony poses for a portrait at a literary festival in Oxford.

Alex Rider is a London boy whose parents work for the British Secret Intelligence Service, MI6. Tragically, his mother and father are both killed by an evil organization, and Alex is taken into the care of his uncle Ian, also a secret agent. Then Ian too is murdered. MI6 pressure Alex into taking over his role, even though he is only 14. Poor Alex is not keen at all, but he turns out to be an extremely intelligent, brave and skilful spy.

As Anthony began to write Alex's story, he knew that 'this would finally be the breakthrough I had been looking for.' Indeed, *Stormbreaker* catapulted its author to worldwide fame.

Anthony Horowitz is now famous as an author of fiction for children and young adults. He has written several successful TV crime series and film scripts too, and his work is popular across the generations.

INSPIRATION

For Anthony, a vital inspiration for Alex Rider was watching James Bond movies as a child. Anthony had always thought it would be brilliant if James Bond became a teenager.

A still from the film of Stormbreaker, *the first Alex Rider novel, showing Alex with his friend Sabina engaged in a daredevil mission to defeat an evil genius.*

Anthony was born in Stanmore, North London on 5 April 1955 into a Jewish family. He lived with his parents and brother and sister in a grand home called White Friars. They had a cook, housemaid, two gardeners, a handyman and a chauffeur (driver).

Yet despite his wealthy background, Anthony's home life was unhappy. As he says, 'Sometimes I think the family I was brought up in was 100 years out of date. A gong would sound to announce a dinner prepared by servants.' At dinner, the children were expected to provide witty conversation. Also, the dinners were huge, so Anthony became overweight.

Anthony's father, Mark, was a **solicitor** and businessman who spent little time with his children. Even though he loved books, he never read with Anthony. Eventually, Mark's business interests failed and he went **bankrupt**. The family had to move to a smaller house with just one housekeeper called Fitzy.

Anthony as a boy. He was not close to his brother or sister, so he often felt lonely.

As a young boy, Anthony spent the most time with his mother, Joyce. She used to read him horror stories at bedtime – a very odd choice for a young child. Yet Anthony adored these bedtime tales, and soon developed a great love of books and reading.

Anthony regularly saw his grandmother, Esther Charatan, but his relationship with her was very difficult and he dreaded her visits. Every Christmas she gave him a big box of chocolates – he always thought it was a rather odd present for an overweight boy. Although Anthony was unhappy at home, the next stage in his life was no improvement.

WOW!

For his 13th birthday, Anthony asked his mother for a human skull – and she bought him one! Joyce was an unusual mother indeed.

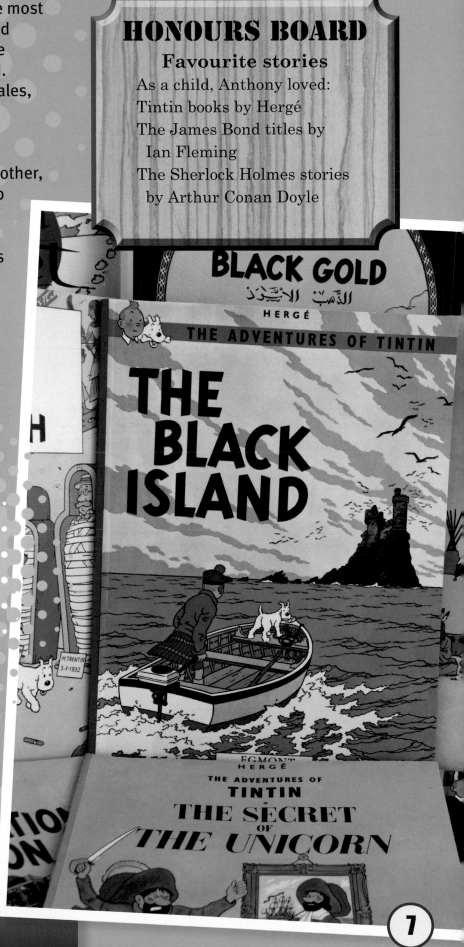
Some covers of Tintin books, which Anthony loved as a boy. He has since visited all the places mentioned in the Tintin books – except the Moon!

At age eight, Anthony was packed off to a private **boarding school**. He hated it. Orley Farm was a typical **prep school** in the 1960s. He thought the teachers were strict and treated the children harshly. Many years later, Anthony would depict the school's headmaster and his wife in a TV episode – as mad Nazis!

Anthony suffered because, as a boy, he was overweight and he was also a slow learner. The teachers made him feel bad about himself. He recalls, 'It was a horrible place. At Orley Farm I had been educated to believe I was completely stupid.'

WOW!

Anthony recalls, 'Once the headmaster told me to stand up in assembly and in front of the whole school said, "This boy is so stupid he will not be coming to Christmas games tomorrow." ' What a terrible way to treat a child!

Today, schools like Orley Farm are very different from how they were in the 1960s. This boy reads by torchlight in bed. For Anthony, books provided a wonderful means of escape from daily life at school.

Reading provided Anthony's escape from daily misery: 'I hated my school and books saved me from it. They were my lifeline,' he remembers. After lights out in the **dormitory**, several other boys would gather round, and Anthony would tell stories. The boys would whisper in the dark in case the staff caught them awake and punished them. Anthony's tales involved two boys, Jimmy and Edward, who were always having exciting adventures.

As young as eight, Anthony already knew he wanted to be a writer. He used to ask for books and pens for his birthday. When he was 10, he wrote a play all about Guy Fawkes, who planned to blow up the **Houses of Parliament** in 1605.

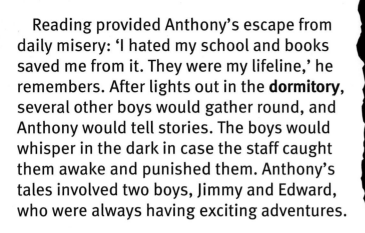

TOP TIP

Anthony advises you to think long and hard about the first sentence of a piece of writing. It is important for grabbing the reader's attention. For example, the first sentence of *Stormbreaker* is 'When the doorbell rings at three in the morning, it's never good news.'

Boys listen to a friend telling a story. Anthony tested out his storytelling skills on his friends and began to write down his tales.

A change for the better

After Orley Farm, Anthony's life took a turn for the better. When he was 13, he started at Rugby School, an expensive private boarding school. Here, students were treated with kindness and respect. At Rugby, Anthony developed his interests in literature, drama and poetry, and read widely. He found opportunities to write for the school newspaper and magazine.

INSPIRATION

At Rugby School, Anthony had three English teachers who encouraged him to read and inspired him to write: Mr Alden, Mr Helliwell and Mr Brown. They introduced him to the 17th-century **playwright** William Shakespeare, and 19th-century authors Jane Austen and Charles Dickens.

At Rugby School (shown here) Anthony became an avid reader. Dickens influenced Anthony the most, with his long, colourful stories and fascinating characters.

Once he had finished school in 1973, Anthony was keen to see the world. He had been cooped up in boarding schools for ten years, and was hungry for new experiences. He decided to have a **gap year** before going to university and flew off to Australia. There he worked for nine months as a cowboy. It was a complete contrast to his previous life.

Back in England again, Anthony went to York University, in northern England, to study English **Literature** and Art History. The atmosphere was relaxed, and he did not have to work particularly hard. He enjoyed writing plays and had lots of fun. In 1977, he **graduated**. What would he do next?

A cowboy in Australia rounds up a cattle. After Australia, Anthony made an adventurous trek back to England, travelling overland through countries such as Afghanistan and Iran.

WOW!

As a cowboy, Anthony learnt to ride a horse, shoot a gun and to butcher cattle and chop them into steaks!

The year 1977 brought a shock to Anthony and his family. His father died of cancer, aged just 60. Mark Horowitz had never believed his son would make it as a writer and had always scoffed at his efforts to write. Now he would never know of his son's remarkable success.

But another trauma was to follow. The wealthy Horowitz family discovered that Mark Horowitz still had vast **debts**. It seemed he had taken all of his money out of the bank and shifted it to a secret Swiss bank account to avoid paying them. However, he had not told anyone in the family how to find the money.

Anthony's mother travelled to Switzerland a few times to try to discover what had happened to the cash, but to no avail. The family's wealth had disappeared into thin air. Joyce was forced to go out to work, and took a job as a secretary for a building company. As it turned out, she enjoyed her new working life.

Mark Horowitz (pictured middle) photographed with other businessmen, in 1966. Although Mark never read with Anthony, he used to discuss his love of books with his son.

INSPIRATION

Anthony's family life influenced his writing. *Stormbreaker* starts with a funeral, inspired by the memories of his father's funeral.

Anthony was now living in London again. He began work as a **copywriter** at the company McCann Erickson. His job was to write advertisements, which he found rather dull. Looking back, he remarks, 'I wish I had used those years to test myself more and to live a little more dangerously.'

Yet there was one positive result of this job: he met his wife Jill Green. Their first date was a business trip to Alton Towers theme park, where they had enormous fun on the rides. They married in Hong Kong in 1988.

Anthony, photographed in 1980, before he became well known. His wife Jill has described him as 'the most creative person I have ever met'.

WOW!

Anthony Horowitz married his boss! At McCann Erickson, Jill was the account manager and he worked for her. It was unusual to have a female manager in the 1970s. Jill later became a TV producer.

While working as a copywriter, Anthony developed his own writing. His first book for children, *Enter Frederick K. Bower*, was published in 1978, when he was 22.

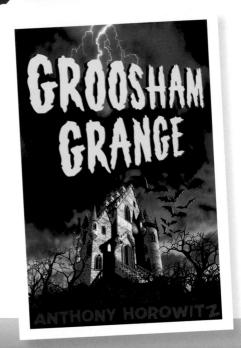

Encouraged, Anthony produced some more titles, including *Misha, the Magician and the Mysterious Amulet*. His early books, about unloving families and horrible schools, drew on the harsh experiences of his childhood. He also wrote a non-fiction title, *The Kingfisher Book of Myths & Legends*. Anthony particularly enjoyed researching Robin Hood, who was featured in the book.

Groosham Grange was not hugely popular when it was first published, but since Anthony has become a celebrated writer, it has gained popularity.

At 30, Anthony left his job in advertising to focus full-time on writing. In 1986, *The Falcon's Malteser* was published, the first of the Diamond Brothers series, featuring teenage detective duo Nick Diamond and his silly brother Tim. Two years later, *Groosham Grange* came out – the central character is David Eliot, a boy with magical powers who attends an academy of witchcraft. This was a decade before J. K. Rowling's first Harry Potter title came out.

HONOURS BOARD

The Diamond Brothers series
These books are old but still popular.
They include:
The Falcon's Malteser, 1986
Public Enemy Number Two, 1987
South by South East, 1991
The French Confection, 2002

INSPIRATION

Anthony draws inspiration from films he loves. He took the title of one of his favourite films, *The Maltese Falcon*, and developed the idea for *The Falcon's Malteser*.

However, Anthony's books had limited success. He decided to try his hand at writing for TV, so he bought a book about how to do it. It just happened that the TV producers of *Robin of Sherwood* were looking for a story, so Anthony wrote a **script** and sent it to them. Fortunately, they liked it, and asked him to write for the series. Things were beginning to look up for Anthony...

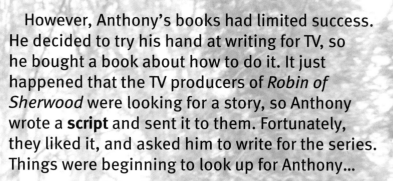

A still from the Robin of Sherwood *TV programme from 1986. It was based on the tales of Robin Hood, who 'stole from the rich to give to the poor'.*

Anthony is passionate about writing. He doesn't see it as work! He explains: 'Sometimes I'll spend 10 or 11 hours on my own in my office...but I won't notice the passing of time and I'll never get bored because I'm immersed in my story.'

First, Anthony carefully plans the **structure** of a book. He sees the shape of the story in his head, with all the twists and turns of the plot. He loves this part – constructing the tale and working out where the detective takes a wrong turn, and when he realizes his errors and goes off another tack. Anthony also makes a list of ingredients: the vital features to include in the story.

Then Anthony handwrites his story in notebooks. After, he transfers it to his computer, **editing** as he types. Writing a book can take up to a year!

TOP TIP

Anthony advises you to 'think about what you're going to write before you sit down and write it.' Spend time planning out the story.

Anthony in his office at home. Even though he is a famous writer, his life has not changed greatly. He still spends most of his days alone in his office, quietly writing.

When not writing, Anthony is often researching his next title. He investigates the subject thoroughly and tries out as many of his characters' experiences as possible. For example, in the second Alex Rider book, *Point Blanc*, Alex commandeers a crane. As background research, Anthony himself climbed a 150-metre (492-foot) crane – even though he's scared of heights! While working on The Power of Five series (see page 22), he dared to visit the dangerous area of Hong Kong where criminal gangs operate.

Anthony Horowitz with his family. They are very close and enjoy working together.

INSPIRATION

All of Anthony's family are involved in his creative work. His wife produces some of his TV scripts. Their older son Nicholas helped to research the Alex Rider books (see page 20) by learning snowboarding and scuba diving. Cassian, their younger son, acted in *Foyle's War* and *Midsomer Murders* – and both sons appeared in *Crime Traveller*.

Anthony's big break

Anthony continued to write children's books in the 1990s. In 1994, *Granny* was published. It was all about evil grannies who hate children and try to steal their youth through a wicked plot. Two years later came *The Switch*, about two boys who swap lives. At this time, Anthony's books contained lots of word play and jokes – some for young readers, others aimed more at adults.

Meanwhile, Anthony's TV writing was going well. After *Robin of Sherwood*, he adapted several Hercule Poirot detective stories by 20th-century crime writer Agatha Christie for television. From 1997, he created the detective series, the *Midsomer Murders*, about a number of murders in the sleepy English countryside. His TV career seemed to be going far better than his children's books. But then the situation changed dramatically.

Anthony with 15-year-old Alex Pettyfer when it was announced that Alex would play Alex Rider in the film of Stormbreaker.

INSPIRATION

Granny was based on the character of Anthony's own grandmother, Esther Charatan!

With the publication in 2000 of *Stormbreaker*, the first Alex Rider book, Anthony knew he had found his voice: 'The character of Alex leapt, fully developed, on to the page.' Alex's first mission is to **infiltrate** a group run by a mad inventor called Herod Sayle. The evil genius is plotting to kill all the schoolchildren in England using chemical weapons delivered through the school computer system. It is up to Alex to stop him.

Stormbreaker is a fast-**paced** adventure story, full of action, spying and gadgets. It was a big hit. The book came out soon after the first Harry Potter title, when publishers were looking for the next author to fire young people's imaginations. *Stormbreaker* proved to be the right book at the right time.

WOW!

Sometimes Anthony puts people who have annoyed him into his books – as nasty characters who come to a sticky end!

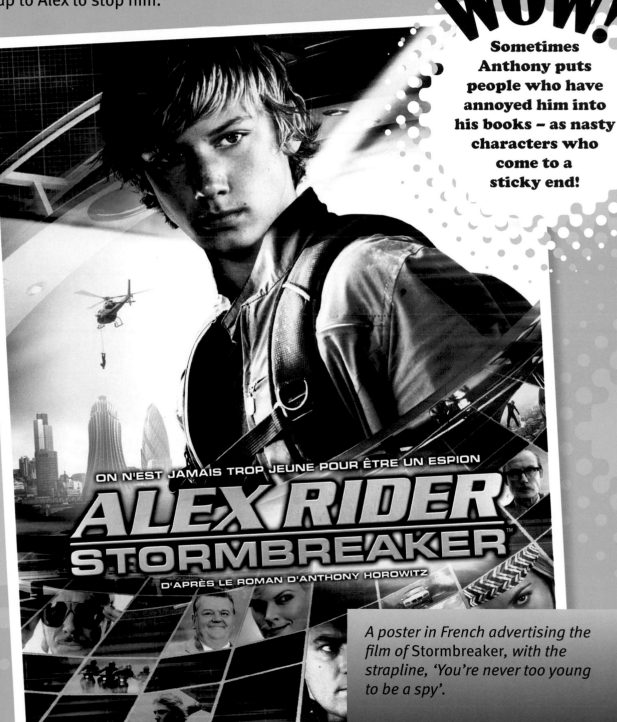

A poster in French advertising the film of Stormbreaker, *with the strapline, 'You're never too young to be a spy'.*

The Alex Rider series

After the tremendous success of *Stormbreaker*, Anthony developed the story into a series of nine books. Throughout the series, Alex carries out missions for MI6 and takes on the worldwide criminal organisation Scorpia. He develops extraordinary talents and survival skills. Against all the odds, he always outwits his cruel, clever adult opponents.

For example, in the second title, *Point Blanc*, Alex is sent to a mysterious boarding school for wealthy boys in the Swiss Alps to investigate the suspicious activities of the headmaster. Once he has discovered the head's evil plot, he has to make a dramatic escape – using an ironing board he has adapted to snowboard down an icy mountain.

Several of the Alex Rider books have been produced in an exciting graphic novel format to widen the appeal of the books even further.

WOW!

The Alex Rider series sold 12 million copies worldwide. The books have been translated into 28 languages.

ALEX RIDER

POINT BLANC
THE GRAPHIC NOVEL
ANTHONY HOROWITZ
Antony Johnston · Kanako and Yuzuru

Unlike James Bond, when Alex experiences danger he is often badly hurt. This makes the stories more believable. The amazing gadgets in the book are another popular feature. They include the drinking straw that contains a knock-out dart (in *Scorpia*) and a spot cream that can eat through metal (*Stormbreaker*). In *Snakehead*, Alex has three special coins that contain explosives for emergency use.

The Alex Rider series had a great impact. One parent, Robin, from Manchester told how 'My son, Noah, who is 8, recently began reading the Alex Rider series and is hooked… we have a nightly discussion about switching off his light because he says they're too exciting to stop reading.' Although Anthony had not set out to write for boys – he simply loves storytelling – Alex's adventures were helping to get boys into reading.

Saving the world one mission at a time

ALEX RIDER
CROCODILE TEARS

ANTHONY HOROWIT
#1 New York Times bestselling author

The cover of the eighth title in the series. In this book, reluctant spy Alex travels between cold London, baking-hot southern India, and East Africa – the home of the vicious African crocodile.

HONOURS BOARD
The Alex Rider series
Stormbreaker, 2000
Point Blanc, 2001
Skeleton Key, 2002
Eagle Strike, 2003
Scorpia, 2004
Ark Angel, 2005
Snakehead, 2007
Crocodile Tears, 2009
Scorpia Rising, 2011

TV, films and more books!

Although he was busy with the Alex Rider series, Anthony wrote several other books in the early 2000s, including some new Diamond Brothers titles.

TOP TIP

Anthony says you should 'write what you want to write', in the way that you like. It could be sad, scary or funny.

ANTHONY
HOROWITZ

THE POWER OF FIVE

RAVEN'S GATE

DARKNESS WAITS ON
THE OTHER SIDE...

In 2005, Anthony introduced The Power of Five, based on an earlier series, The Gatekeepers, which Anthony had written back in the 1980s. The theme again was special children, but this time they had **supernatural** powers. Anthony was fascinated by the idea of astonishing events going on close to home. He used to wonder, 'Why does so much **fantasy** have to be foreign?...Isn't it more exciting to imagine these great battles... happening in the very high street where you live...just out of the corner of your eye?'

In Raven's Gate, *the first of the* Power of Five *series, the hero Matt Freeman is sent to an odd foster mother in Yorkshire and finds himself embroiled in a battle against devil-worshippers.*

Anthony's TV work continued too. In 2002, his *Foyle's War* series was launched, about a British detective tackling crime during the Second World War. Produced by Anthony's wife Jill, it was hugely successful. Later dramas for TV included *Collision* (2009) and *Injustice* (2011).

He entered the movie world too, writing the **screenplay** for *The Gathering*, a horror film in 2005 starring Christina Ricci. Anthony has always loved horror stories. The following year, he **adapted** *Stormbreaker* for the screen, the first-ever Alex Rider film.

Anthony even found time to write a novel for adults, *The Killing Joke*, and to write plays: *Mindgame*, a thriller for the theatre, and the comedy *A Handbag*. He was enjoying an extremely busy and fulfilling career.

HONOURS BOARD

Some of Anthony's awards

- Winner of Lew Grade Audience award, BAFTA, 2003, for *Foyle's War*.
- British Book Awards Children's Book of the Year in 2006 for *Ark Angel*.
- Author of the Year at the British Book Industry Awards, 2007.

Anthony at the Crime Thrillers awards in London in 2010, at which Foyle, the hero of Foyle's War, *was voted the UK's favourite TV detective.*

After nine books, Anthony finally said goodbye to Alex Rider. To finish the final title, *Scorpia Rising*, he travelled to his house on the river in Orford, Suffolk. He wrote the last words at sunset. Although the book is dark and sad, it ends with hope.

Anthony at the launch of Ark Angel *in 2005. After finishing the Alex Rider series, Anthony said he would write just a few more children's books.*

TOP TIP

If you're a budding writer, try to read as much as possible. It's good to read books from start to finish to learn how to structure a piece of writing.

When *Scorpia Rising* was published in 2011, fans asked if there might be more Alex Rider books. *Russian Roulette*, a book about the killer Yassen Gregorovich, who features in the series, was released in 2013, but Anthony will not write any further Alex Rider stories. He believes it is best to end a series on a high and not to write that extra book that spoils the set.

In 2011, Anthony was working as hard as ever, writing the final title in The Power of Five series, the sequel to the Tintin film *The Secret of the Unicorn*, and a 10-part TV drama, *Yellow Gold*.

That same year, *The House of Silk* came out. This was Anthony's Sherlock Holmes novel for adults. Many Sherlock Holmes stories have appeared since Arthur Conan Doyle published the last Sherlock Holmes title in 1927, but Anthony was the first to write with the approval of the Conan Doyle estate, the group owned by the author's family that protects his work. Sherlock Holmes fans welcomed the new title.

INSPIRATION

Inspiration comes more easily if you can identify with your subject. To write the Tintin sequel, Anthony drew on the Tintin books he loved as a boy. Tintin is a reporter, and reading his adventures made Anthony want to write and travel the world.

An illustration of Tintin and Captain Haddock at a Hergé exhibition in Paris in 1987. The Secret of the Unicorn *helped to bring the Tintin stories to a new generation of children.*

Helping charities

Anthony uses his position as a popular author to help charities. Since 2009, he has been an ambassador of East Anglia Children's Hospices, a charity in eastern England that helps terminally ill children – young people that have an illness or condition that will cause them to die.

Anthony is also a **patron** of Kidscape, a charity that works to prevent bullying. He was bullied as a child because of his weight, so he knows what it feels like and likes to help children who suffer bullying today.

He also undertakes **outreach work** with youth offenders (children who have committed crimes) and looked after children (those who live in children's homes) to encourage them to read.

A girl is helped by a care assistant at the East Anglia Children's Hospice. As an ambassador, Anthony helps to promote the work of the charity and assists in raising funds.

Because of his outreach work, in 2008 Anthony was made the first Champion Author for the National Year of Reading, which was launched that year to promote reading for pleasure in the family. He believes that reading should be fun and has taken part in events to promote it.

In October 2011, for example, Anthony helped the Read for the Royal National Institute for the Blind (RNIB) Day, which raises money to assist people who have lost their sight to enjoy books. To gain **publicity**, the RNIB decided to try to beat the world record for **relay reading**. On the day, 317 people gathered in London and took it in turns to read lines from Anthony's new Diamond Brothers short story, *The Double Eagle has Landed*. They easily beat the previous world record of 290 people!

WOW!

By 2011, Anthony had written about 5 million words altogether!

TOP TIP

Anthony says that it is good to think of a title for your story that will entice people to read it: 'The secret is to bring powerful words together in an unusual way. For example the words SKELETON + KEY make a good book title.'

The RNIB gathering that beat the world relay-reading record. On the day, the book was made available in standard print, large print and Braille (a reading system created for blind people).

The Impact of Anthony Horowitz

Anthony has developed a successful writing formula. His books grab the readers' attention from the first sentence. The text is easy to read, the pace is fast and there is plenty of **suspense**, so readers do not get bored. Anthony works hard to keep a good balance in his writing – his readers will encounter violence, threat and danger, but not so much that they will have nightmares!

The main characters are heroic and attractive yet they are human and have their faults. Readers come to know them and care what happens in their lives. This helps to maintain interest throughout the series. Also, the books become more demanding as the series goes on, so the reader develops with them.

Anthony signing copies of Snakehead, *from the Alex Rider series. He enjoys meeting his young readers, and sometimes he uses their names in his books!*

Anthony's story writing has persuaded children who have never picked up a book before to enter the world of books – and to keep reading. As one London teacher told him, 'You have turned on so many "turned-off" students to reading with the Alex Rider books.' The popularity of Anthony's books has spread internationally, particularly in the USA. The author has many adult fans as well as young readers.

WOW!

Anthony has written chase scenes involving all kinds of vehicles in his children's books. *The House of Silk* gave him the opportunity to write a horse and carriage chase scene!

Anthony has had an enormous impact on film and TV too, writing some of the most popular series on British TV. He has been described as a 'one-stop crime shop' for his TV work. With his ability to write for a variety of media, it is clear that Anthony Horowitz is one of the most successful writers in the UK.

Anthony (pictured centre) and other well-known children's authors at a World Book Day celebration in 2007. Every year, World Book Day encourages children to discover the joys of reading.

Have you got what it takes to be a writer?

1) Would you describe yourself as imaginative?
a) No, I prefer dealing with what's happening in the here and now.
b) Yes, I enjoy reading and imagining other peoples' lives.
c) Definitely! I'm constantly inventing stories in my head.

2) Which best describes your reading habits?
a) I read when I have to for school work.
b) I sometimes read books or magazines for pleasure.
c) I'm always reading – I'll read anything and everything.

3) It's raining and you're planning an afternoon with your friends. What do you suggest?
a) Playing outdoors – a bit of rain never hurt anyone.
b) Computer games.
c) Word games! I love all kinds of word play.

4) When you have to do some writing work for homework...
a) I leave it until the last minute because I don't enjoy it.
b) I get on with it, write it quickly and hand it in.
c) I plan it carefully and allow time to edit and refine it before handing it in.

5) You are invited to a creative writing workshop. What do you do?
a) I make my excuses. It's not for me!
b) I think about it and decide to have a go.
c) I sign up straight away. I'd like to get some expert advice on the stories I'm writing.

6) If someone criticizes your writing, how do you respond?
a) I don't take much notice.
b) I get a little upset but don't change how I work.
c) I take the criticism seriously and make note of the points for my next writing assignment.

RESULTS

Mostly As: You don't seem very keen on writing at the moment. Try to find books to read on topics that you like – either fiction or non-fiction. Then you might feel inspired to start writing.

Mostly Bs: You clearly have an interest in reading and writing. Try to read widely and see if you can spend some more time on your writing.

Mostly Cs: You may have what it takes to be a writer! Continue to read as widely as possible and get into a routine of writing regularly. See if you can join a writing group for support.

adapt To change a book so that it can be made into a film or TV programme.

bankrupt Without enough money to pay what you owe.

boarding school A school where students live during term time.

copywriter A person whose job it is to write the words for advertisements.

debt A sum of money that a person owes.

dormitory A room where several people sleep.

editing Correcting the mistakes in a piece of writing and improving it.

fantasy Books that use magic or the supernatural as the main theme.

gap year A year between school and university when some students work or travel.

graduated Gained a degree at university.

Houses of Parliament The London buildings where the British Parliament makes laws.

infiltrate To enter a place or organization secretly.

literature Pieces of writing, such as novels, plays and poems, that are thought to be of high quality.

outreach work The activity of an organization that provides a service to people where they live.

pace In writing, making sure that events happen at just the right pace leaving the readers wanting to know more.

patron A well-known person who has a personal interest in the charity and helps to raise awareness of its work.

playwright A person who writes plays.

prep school A private school for children aged 7 to thirteen.

producer The person in charge of the practical and funding side of making a television programme.

publicity Making something known to the public, such as a new book.

relay reading When people take it in turns to read a piece of work.

screenplay The words for a film with directions as to how it should be acted and filmed.

script The written text of a play, film or TV programme.

scriptwriting Writing the text for a play, film or TV programme.

solicitor A lawyer who advises people on legal matters.

structure The way in which writing is organized, such as the chapters and scenes.

supernatural Something that cannot be explained by the laws of science and seems to involve gods or magic.

suspense A feeling of excitement when you don't know what is going to happen next.